WHAT WAS IT

before it was

bread?

by Jane Belk Moncure

illustrated by Elizabeth Nygaard

THE CHILD'S WORLD

ELGIN, ILLINOIS 60120

Distributed by Childrens Press, 1224 West Van Buren Street, Chicago, Illinois 60607.

Library of Congress Cataloging in Publication Data

Moncure, Jane Belk.
  What was it before it was bread?

  (A let's find out book)
  Summary: Traces the process by which wheat is grown, cut, ground into different kinds of flour, and baked into bread. Includes a recipe for whole wheat muffins.
    1. Bread—Juvenile literature. 2. Grain—Juvenile literature. [1. Wheat. 2. Flour. 3. Bread. 4. Bakers and bakeries] I. Nygaard, Elizabeth, ill. II. Title. III. Series.
TX769.M623 1985   664'.7523   85-11402
ISBN 0-89565-323-0

1 2 3 4 5 6 7 8 9 10 11 12 R 91 90 89 88 87 86 85

John eats a slice of wheat bread and
asks, "What was my bread before it was
bread? How does the grocery store get its
bread? Where does bread come from?"
Let's find out.

It all starts when a farmer plants tiny seeds of wheat. The seeds are so tiny you can hold hundreds of them in one hand.

The seeds grow roots, stems, and leaves. At first the plants look just like grass.

Then the plants grow tall in the
sunshine and rain. At the tops of the
wheat stems, berry-like grains grow.

Slowly, the wheat field turns from
green to yellow and then to gold.

Then it is time for the farmer to cut the wheat—not with a little lawn mower, but with a machine as big as a dinosaur.

Next the wheat is loaded on
trucks . . .

and taken to a flour mill.

At the mill, the hard grains are washed in huge tubs.

Then they are poured into giant
machines that roll and crush, crack and
pound them into smaller and smaller
pieces until they become soft flour.

The whole-wheat flour is golden brown.

But some flour is made with only parts of the wheat grains. That flour is white.

After the flour is sifted, and put into bags, off it goes to a bakery.

There the flour is poured into a
giant mixing machine.

17

Inside the mixing machine, a large egg beater mixes and mixes it with other good things—honey, butter, milk, eggs.

When the mixture comes out of the
machine, it is bread dough—lots and
lots of bread dough.

The dough is cut into lumps and put into pans . . . row by row by row.

The pans are popped into an oven as
big as your kitchen! When the pans
come out, the bread is golden brown.

You can smell the freshly baked bread
as it is sliced and wrapped and packed.

Then a bakery truck takes the bread
to grocery stores—all kinds of grocery
stores.

So now we know what John's bread
was before it was bread. It was golden
wheat growing in a wheat field far
away.

Plus Pages

Here is the circle story you have read . . . from seeds of wheat to whole-wheat bread.

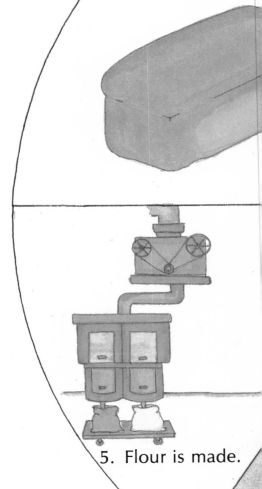

6. Bread is baked.

5. Flour is made.

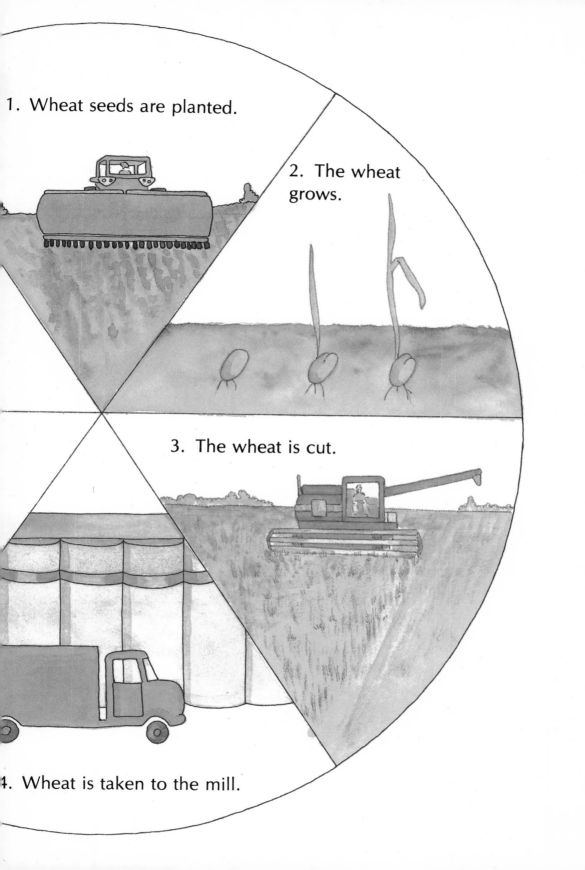

1. Wheat seeds are planted.

2. The wheat grows.

3. The wheat is cut.

4. Wheat is taken to the mill.

Many other good things are made at the bakery from wheat flour, including . . .

cookies,

cupcakes,

doughnuts,

buns,

birthday cakes,

crackers,

cereal,

spaghetti,

pancake mix,

macaroni,

and muffins.

You can make your own whole-wheat muffins.
Here's how.

1. Mix in a large bowl:

   2 cups of whole wheat flour

   with 1 tablespoon of baking powder.

2. Now add 3 eggs,

   ¼ cup of milk,    ½ stick of soft butte[r]

   ¼ cup of honey.

3. Stir only until the dough is wet.

4. Spoon into 12 paper muffin cups. (Do not fill to the top.)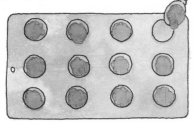

5. Bake in oven (425°) for 18 minutes or until golden brown.

People all around the world eat bread
every day—bread made not only from
wheat, but from other grains such as:

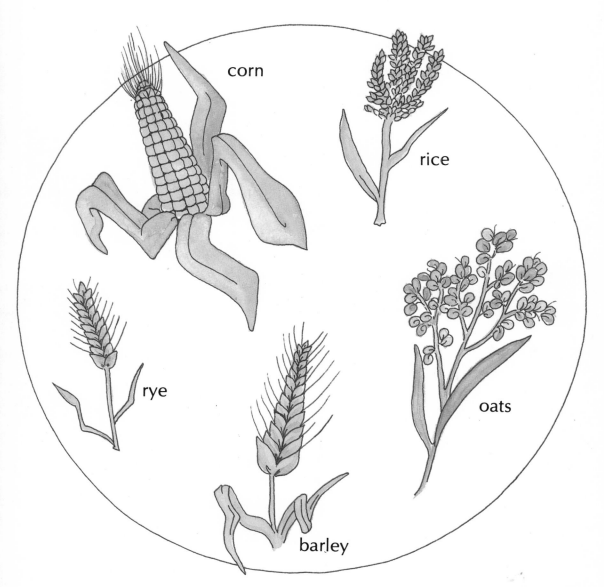

corn

rice

rye

oats

barley

Bread is good food for everyone,
everywhere.